Tracy Patrick was b_
poetry slams in Glasg_
involved with theatre a_   _s with
the world's oldest surviv_   _ie Britannia
Panopticon. Her first poe   _illet, *Wild Eye Fire
Eye*, was published in 201_, and was followed in 2019
by her debut novel, *Blushing is for Sinners*, which was
commended by the Saltire First Book of the Year
award judges, and named by the late Ruby McCann as
one of *The Bottle Imp*'s best Scottish books of 2019.

tracypatrick.org

Also by Tracy Patrick

Novel
BLUSHING IS FOR SINNERS

Poetry Pamphlet
WILD EYE FIRE EYE

PORTRAIT

Tracy Patrick

earth love

First published in 2022 by earth love press
earthlovepoetrymagazine@yahoo.com

All rights reserved. No reproduction, copy or transmission of this publication may be made without the prior written permission of the publisher.

Copyright © Tracy Patrick, 2022
Tracy Patrick has asserted her moral right to be identified as the author of this work.

A catalogue record for this book is available from the British Library.

ISBN 978-1-7397044-0-7

Cover painting by Louise Malone
Cover design by earth love press
Typeset by earth love press in Baskerville Old Face

Printed and bound by Imprint Academic
Seychelles Farm, Upton Pyne, Exeter, Devon, EX5 5HY

Dedicated to

The NHS doctors, nurses and staff, and the passers-by
in the street without whose compassion and quick
thinking I would not be here. Thank you.

CONTENTS

CLOVER

I wonder where
you found it, the
four-leafed clover
you gave me one
birthday, or was
it Easter – the
one you framed in
plastic from a
chocolate egg box,
or was it a
ready-meal – a
kind of clover
reliquary
which I taped to
the back of a
pocket notepad,
or was it a
diary – with a
pink-green floral
cover, transferred
it year after
year until one
day I ran out
of diaries, or
was it luck? So
I thank you for
the gift of the
four-leafed clover.
It's difficult
to measure its
effectiveness.

In any case
I'm here, and it's
the thought that counts.

INCUBATOR

Like an embryo
it's lost without a body to be in.
The tiny rhythm
of its beating is a child trying its
very best to be
good. It knows it is up for adoption,
wants to make a nice
impression. There will be no shortage of
homes, of those who want
to hold it close, tell it that everything
is going to be
fine. A heart must be loved and treated well
by a parent who
understands the anxiety of losing
a body. Till then
it is warmed, fed, would leap its walls for the
life it has to give.

A PROCEDURE

cauterised nerves   curtained stage   secret inventory
        sharpened blade

voluntary signature   blindfolded choice
wheeled destiny
        expectant audience

absent drum   fluorescent sun   first throw
        small gash

the warm claret
on lambent flesh
the opening like a mouth
too small for my hand
to reach in
and feel the pulse

here is your card

curtained table   cauterised destiny   involuntary throw
        stitched pocket

LESSONS OF FIRE

All this rushing with water
will only disappoint.

A way must be cleared,
fire nurtured and encouraged.

We should learn to
handle fire at an early age.

Combustion is crucial
to our central nervous system.

Confessions are delivered
in its chaste tongue.

My own pen incinerates
at the end of a dishonest sentence.

For the most part it is helpful,
teaches you to try again.

Lightning rods are also good,
bare feet, buckets of sand.

CROSSHATCHING

coming out of a fug
people in my front room
how did they get there
one of them writing on the walls
beam me up scotty
a silhouette behind the curtain
just standing there
not saying anything
a man in the bathroom
piercing his groin
with a syringe
our eyes meet   barely seeing
where was I before   this
a flat above the subway
a woman pushed
through the window
glass shattering in slow motion
her body suspended
by his fist   the cloth of her jacket
a horizontal eternity
then
dancing   beer   snorting
a man shooting into his groin
the same one
and before that   where was I
hard to say
rewind to throwing up
on a street corner
tightening the tourniquet
the strange comfort of it   eyes
closing   peaceful   sinking

downwards   always easier
going down
somewhere there are armfuls
of diamonds
who needs light
it all happens   underground
where shadows
become your friends
and you wonder   what you were
so afraid   of
violence   is merely another dance
to be learned practised
soon you will have it perfect
nothing is ugly it's all horizontal
universal   where was I
before this   I was too upright
sore from standing
my back ached   trying too hard
to remember   things
as though they mattered
all of it   forward propulsion
instead of down
begin where you began
in the dark   the worms are translucent
they glitter like diamonds
nuggets of glass in the earth
the coolness of the tomb
comforting not empty   at all
but full   of dancing shadows
my pupils have given birth
to gods   I see them everywhere
they have perfect veins
that wriggle when touched

and a ticklish sense of humour
I have discovered
my origins and they are smiling
as they fall   backwards
waiting for something   to give way
the crack in the pavement
a place to slip between
there are people in my room
there will be violence
it is coming   vertical   threats   a fear
of being upright   of standing
of walking   too straight

ALARM CALL

They stand around my bed at five am
Dressed in dark blue slacks and polo shirts
And belts with radios attached
Amidst the static crackling a disembodied voice
Refers to me as a client
They switch on the light and talk loudly
Into my face
Tracy   Tracy   Tracy
Are you okay
Tracy
Are you okay
I'm beginning to register
Who they are and what they want
How did they get here
Inside my room
Yes I'm okay
Are you sure
Don't take me away
To the place for the dispossessed
Those who live but have ceased to live
Tracy, you pressed the button didn't you
What button
I wonder if there's anything to be gained by lying
I was troubled in my dreams
A subconscious desire to see other human beings
For their chattering business-like bodies
To pass over my field of vision
For their confusing and comforting forms
To be within my empty walls
Radio frequencies click and hiss in the morning dusk
Am I coming through

9

Yes. I read you. False alarm. It was an accident. I
    repeat. An accident
I'm sorry
It's okay, Tracy, we get this all the time
You're not the first and you won't be the last
Ha ha
So, you're alright
Yes
Well we will leave you then
Now
Yes
The door shuts
Vacant air
I'm sorry
Not the last
I'm sorry
Not

PROXIMATIONS

It permeates my seams
like the mustiness of old furniture,
dullness of second-hand wood.

I stand waiting
in the supermarket queue
or the trendy café that plays electronica,
walk along the train platform
in new shoes
and designer thrift shop clothes,
I memorise poetry
in an effort to hide it,
to fool them all –

but everyone knows
I am an actor trying too hard
to act,
my entrances and exits slightly
off cue,
my gestures a touch
delayed;
instead of listening
they are thinking of those jellyfish
who wind up on the beach,
how their colour drains
in the sun
and I am thinking of the bloodied rabbit
I almost avoided
on the side of the motorway and how
I couldn't turn back, too scared
to see it twitching.

I think of these things
and do not know why.
My chest is guilty,
full of what I am unable to confess.

Some days I daren't take off my underwear.
I dream of being naked in the woods,
hunter or hunted, it is immaterial,
everything takes me by surprise:
the dappled clearing,
the tree branch and swinging rope,
the sudden suspension
of my slowly-beating heart.

RASKOLNIKOV'S DREAM

Who would you rather be,
the horse or the master?

And which of these has the greater strength,
he who holds the whip

or he who takes the beating?
Even a god is envious

of those who kick
though their knees buckle.

RUMOUR

The thing I am speaking of
is in this box.
Open it and pass it to the next person along.
Now watch each face,
how some will shake their head,
turn pale,
and others nod or
raise a questioning brow.
A few will smile,

but all when asked
will swear to something different:
a lover's bracelet,
a shell picked from a beach,
a child's shoe,
the scent of honeysuckle,
the opening bars of a song –
some will tell a lie
that they think is important,
claim it was nothing – a tale.

It is not for us to say
who is right or wrong,
or whether all is subjective,
but when it is your turn
could you correctly predict the thing
and, if so, would you admit
the difference between what is revealed
and what there is to know?

THE BETA CHART

This small white moon
Will create an area of low pressure

Winds can be breezy at first
Expect an amount of holding onto lampposts

It is advisable to carry an umbrella
It will help steady the nerves

Don't worry about the plodding clouds
They may look like they're sinking

    But there will always be an area of lightness
    Between them and the ground

Breathe it in, think of sliced lemons and salt-washed air
If you find the current is slow or the body

Sluggish, this is because you are at the centre
Of the low. For others, there may be rain

A neon light that blinks but doesn't quite
Go out. You may feel surrounded

By men in heavy grey trench coats
This is called the depression

To escape, turn clockwise or anti-clockwise
Depending on your hemisphere

Listen for your inner narrator – do not be afraid to
    wake them up –
After a while the cycle will become familiar

Like a river draining and filling
Or the tide, a steady matter of clockwork

CRATERS

signs   of   impact
scars   on   the   face   of   the   moon
invisible   from   a   distance
so   you   have   togetcloseup
     enough   to   understand

light   does   not   gather   inside
craters
     they   are   private   places
where   shadow   accumulates
     gravity ——————▶ attracts   trouble
   leaves   nothing   in   the   universe
          undamaged

i   would   like   to   have   seen   the   earth
when   it   was   new
preparing for   life   like   a   body
   fresh   out   of   the   shower

i   am   unsure   about   my   own   gravity
would   like   to   float   weightless
unanchored   escape   the   debris   that   orbits
   the   poles   of   my   mind   and
that   strikes   with   accuracy   in
such   unerring   cycles

17

PERSUASIONS

When you ask me how
I am and I say
resurrected, is that fine?
Of course, you must
assume I am lying, that I
did not wake up in a
cave after three days
being nailed to a cross.
Now that you mention it
I have seen the stone
and nothing can
describe its great
immovability, how it
blocks the light so fully,
seals everything in and
out. Not even Sisyphus
(him again) could give it
a go. His stone is a mere
pebble to be juggled. He
let me feel the weight of
it once and I'd been as
fooled as him. Do you
believe me when I say
that this earth weighs less
than a feather and a
feather weighs more
than earth? Planetary
rock that seals the tomb,
it is true some days I
doubt my own
existence. I am only a

conjurer's fancy, the woman behind the curtain: now you see her, now you don't. Dead Sea salt keeps me afloat. I clutch the philosopher's gold in both my hands and sleep in a council house on a bed of lotus flowers under a druid's sickle. I am Frankenstein's spark. I sit cross-legged on a pin. I am dizzy from falling. My ears hear such soft persuasions. This resurrection is very difficult to explain. I don't know how I can stand it. I have no patience for words. I am afraid to orgasm. Nor can I run through the streets. Sometimes I think it is a sentence, that Lazarus was being polite not to offend. He must have had a hard time explaining his presence at the local inn. Take it from me it tends to overload the living.

Best tell a joke instead,
and keep on ticking until
the rock finally rolls and
not a feather can slip in
between. And if they ask
you   how   you   are,
answer: *Fine.*

SEVENTEEN

I'm a haiku
trying to live my life in
seventeen syllables
or less
and without using verbs
on this occasion
I've failed

BY PROXY

I am taking the train to you, father,
to discuss matters of the heart.
Mine is suspended by a wire,
wakes me at night with stops and starts,
something to do with the genes.
Father, I want to tell you that
there are other ways to communicate,
Ouija boards for example or
that old cliché, a dream.
Send an angel, an incompetent one
in a battered coat, have a song played
on the radio or, if that is too old-fashioned,
summon a YouTube algorithm,
well-timed, to remind me of you –
but not *Caroline* by Status Quo;
yet you choose this, both of us failing to keep time,
and here I am living
the life you don't – it is impossible now
to wish you away so here you stay,
or perhaps it is I who have arrived home.

ERYNGIUM ALPINUM

You bear it all silently
The way a mountain holds up clouds
Or sky provides a view for the bird.
I do not know what name to give to your pain.
A mother's endurance is many thorned.
I want to ask how you hold your back straight
Under the weight of so much loss
And what is that word your lips repeat.
But you hold up a finger, say it clearly and without panic.
Sshh.

DRIFTWOOD

One of these days
I will make something of you,
after I come upon you, accidentally, of course
(for everything that is meant happens by accident),
washed up on a windy shore, your body dipped in waves,
misshapen as a broken arm.
I will drag you along the sand
(for you will weigh next to nothing, a shadow
of your former self),
and take you back to a small beach hut that I own,
filled with things I have collected – bells, beads, raven wings,
old kettles hanging from beams, and rugs from the
     dumpster.
I live alone there, the locals put up with me
because I attract tourists, selling windchimes made from
     shells
(even the sea has become a cliché).
I will place you in a corner of the room,
dry you out day by day, study your form,
how one curve flows into another,
break you into shapes,
work out which is the right way up, if any.
After the first week you will start to speak
in sounds only I can hear,
as loud as a bud when it turns to leaf.
Together we will work out a name,
fill in the blanks you have forgotten.
You will guide my eyes, my hand,
smoothing the skelfs, the rough edges
to the shape that is waiting,
the one you were always meant to be.

THE GREAT MOON

did ye see the moon last night
the great moon
well it wisny that great
it wis mair that it wis
Aye
really bright
as if sumbody had turned it right up
like they wur lookin fur something they lost
and they needed the moon
tae light that wee bit o space doon oan earth
whaur it's too daurk tae see
and tonight I suppose it'll be
back tae normal
but naw it wis a bricht moon
but no that big
and I widny say that it wis great
jist
Aye

SELF-SUFFICIENT

sitting on the white sands
she is there and I am here

watching the sea
rasp against the rocks

also a crow and an imagination
a grey sky with a single flat cloud

she sits and I sit

no one to want or give
no one to know our thoughts

I would like to hear words
form in the ocean's mouth

sand
sea
rock
crow
imagination
sky
cloud
thought
word
ocean
mouth

for the waves to speak our name
tell us what will happen   next

WARHOL WORDS

Land really is the best art
To land on your feet
Requires that you fall
The right way up

The best art is to land, really
With your knees bent
Touching the earth like a cat
Toes spread for balance

Really, art is the best land
No one likes looking at a scrapheap
But underneath each rusted hulk
Is a seed

Is the best land really art
Everything is matter, a matter of opinion
Depends on how you look at it –
Constructed, deconstructed into

land   art   best   really   is   the

C:\> FIELDS

Starting MS-DOS 1.0...
Welcome to MS-DOS
C:\Documents and settings\cd...
C:\dir
Directory of C:\

06/10/2021	03:59	PM	Remember when this was all
01/01/2021	10.01	AM	AUTOEXEC.BAT
11/07/2020	12.33	PM <DIR>	Batch_upload
27/03/2020	03.19	PM	CONFIG.SYS

C:\Fields
Bad command or file name
C:\Car parks

15/07/1981	02.48	PM	We had such fond times in that multi-storey
08/09/1981	01.52	PM	Those were the days
13/10/1981	12.14	PM	Real life catalytic converters
20/04/1982	05.27	PM	Blood and grease

C:\Fields
Bad command or file name
C:\Documents and settings\My Downloads...
C:\Fields
Abort, retry, fail?_
C:\Horizontal green thing surrounded by vertical green things
Invalid file
C:\Horses and carts ploughed the
Restore system to default?

11/05/2022	11.33	AM	DEBUG.TXT
19/11/2022	05.55	AM <DIR>	Program Files

C:\Green

Do you want to upload content?

C:\Archives\grass>pasture>meadow>sward

Not indexed

C:\html # 008000

Select files to delete based on attributes

C:\dir\History

00/00/0000	00.00	AM	All rights reserved
			C:\Consumes carbon
05/08/2025	06.20	PM	Convert I to pure algorithm
03/10/2025	04.17	PM	No carbon footprint
24/01/2026	01.52	PM	Best thing since sliced daily alimentation
31/07/2027	12.14	PM	Who needs chicken feed
06/04/2028	07.38	PM	Bed and board banished
17/02/2029	09.09	AM	No more worrying about funerals
27/11/2029	03.22	AM	Cyber insurance required

C:\Documents and settings\first person singular

Format failure

C:\I am

Retry?

C:\Last known good configuration

01.01.1987	08.51	PM	Input user

C:\Users\Desktop\fields>copy

Format fields

C:\Green

Volume in drive has no label

C:\DOSTEST>dir

29

Testing extended memory?
None
Enter date (mm-dd-yy):
Enter time:
Field not recognised>?
... Increase resolution (SVGA only)
Error
Tab...... Write screen to GIF file
Home...... Go to first screen
Error
End...... Go to last screen
Error
Err
Er
C:\>
C:\
C:
C
?

NEWTON WOODS

We must have circled it
a dozen times
those summer months,
scouring old maps
trying to decipher
that dry Brythonic tongue.

Its murmurs teased us
with faint pronunciations
far down the ravine.
We swept the rocks for runes,
signposts, places where a saint
might rest his bones,

but they were tight-lipped teachers
those old trees,
so we waited until summer
was past and gold
papered the pathways,
revealing branches of invisible ink.

Each half-heard rhyme led us
towards a distant babbling
and we scrabbled on bottoms
down the dark descent,
our fingernails deep in moss.

There we howked the leaves
from his stony throat,
unclogged his lips,
let the words flow into their grail,

and dipped our hands,
cool enough to baptise,
grateful for miracles.

NICHES

1

Because the sun will never be in this position again.

Because I will never look over that tenement roof and
    see Haley's comet or stand in that close-mouth and
    watch the lunar eclipse turn the sky ochre-red.

Because that cat will never again sleep on the roof of
    that hut.

Because he will not lie this way with his arm around me
    on a topaz evening while the night breathes.

Because I will not see the tops of streetlights below our
    window or set this plant on that table or answer that
    landline to a friend.

    Now they are all gone with only a thin skin to
    keep them.

2

Because again I climb the old stairs full of anticipation
    to a place I no longer recognise.

Because the wallpaper is ugly and the bedroom occupied
    by strangers.

Because there is a mouldy growth on the walls and a
    stale smell that would make you vomit.

Because it is the stench of disappointment.

Because they stare blankly and ask what I am doing here.

Because I always try to explain myself when I shouldn't.

    See this is my niche and I have the keys to prove it.

3

Because even while I am talking I know it's too late.

Because my lease was typed on a manual typewriter.

Because I recognise nothing.

Because it was wrong to come back.
Because I am a trespasser in my own past.
Because the distant rushing in my ears is like an
    oncoming wave.
Because I am afraid of drowning
    Because there is always a because.

SLOGANS OF REBELLION

Like saints attempting to explain
THE FAILURE OF GOD
We insist upon a language
That is no longer recognised

Outside the museum's opening hours
Queues wave HANDS OFF MY SUPRA-NATURAL
POST-NIHILIST INHERITANCE placards
Notable in their appreciation of murder
As the one true path

THE ONLY CERTAINTY IS INSANITY –
Or so the essayists tell us –
OUR FINEST DREAMS WILL TAKE PLACE
AT SOME POINT IN THE FUTURE

Until then we must learn to
ANSWER WITH SILENCE
Anything else admits guilt –
TO REBEL IS TO RECOGNISE YOU ARE AT
    FAULT

The new contract states
THERE SHALL BE NO REBELLION
WHILE PROFIT IS IN MOTION
The ruling council will sanction
All necessary executions

A STATE IS ONLY AS GOOD AS ITS PEOPLE
And soon we will all be Darwinian refugees
Waiting for progress

Extinction our just reward

ALL ART THAT DOES NOT FORWARD OUR AIMS
WILL BE DEFINED AS PURPOSELESS
Art must glorify God or us
But never itself

HISTORY FEARS ART
ALMOST AS MUCH AS IT FEARS REBELLION
Because art is neither one thing
Nor the other
And borrows from the museum
Without reverence

Only rebellion –
That constant adjudicator –
Puts a limit on freedom
Or has the power to CANCEL PARADISE
Pronounce it as fallible
As all bad endings

In the depths of the earth
There are fossils
Heroic imprints
That we put in display cases
To remind us of that final stare
Into the void

Whose evolutionary mouths
Pronounce that politics and religion
Are only the surface scum
And that nothing is worth rebelling against
Except the simple fact of death

Wherein we search for that one insoluble
Unshakeable
DOUBT

thinking

reflect ponder ruminate (odd) process digest rationalise
(variable) consider (odd) muse (odd) daydream dream
(odd) name (odd) differentiate (definitely odd) discern
dissect figure guess (there's always one) render
appreciate connect formulate (odd) recognise (odd)
remember (uneven) recall deduce plot (perplex) reason
meditate (unequable) imagine (infinitely divisible)

DIVINATION

Work oot when ye're gony dee
bi timesin the nummer o times ye've been in love
bi the nummer o times nummer is wrate in the Bible,
subtract the nummer o freckles oan yer body
times the nummer o years ye've been abuin the muild
an divide yon bi the colour o yer een
(three fur blue; twa fur broon; four fur green; ither:
    nineteen).
Cannie in't it?

SOUNDING

The temptation is for ship metaphors
but I refuse to liken myself to a hull
or compare my body to the inevitable wreck blown off
    course.

To hell with Sirens and the sea, they are nothing to me.
I have stared into the water's depths, its dead eye.

That is not where you will find me. I am up here
on the cliff, without fear of heights.

The birds do not know what to make of me.
Occasionally one stops to look, on his way somewhere,
senses the thing in me that is broken,

as though there were no cliff under my feet
and I had floated like oil to the surface of a starless void.

It terrifies him.
He does not know what to utter, averts his gaze, flies.

MisantHrOPE

Too damned tough my heart
Punches like a fist calloused
By false warranties
Aggravating to keep sweet
Seeks clichés nevertheless

ANOTHER NIGHT

Why do they disturb me
these mountains

as if they wait for night
to surround me with their stony reproofs.

Yes, I delayed the inevitable
with my endless talk and drink and talk,

and it is true I remember none of it,
words layered upon smoke.

But I have grown to love now
this indifferent silence.

So mountains cease your drums,
it is limited, this certainty of yours.

HOW TO BE AN ARSEHOLE

taps aff
tattoos oot ·
blue bag
cairry oot
get a burd
raise yer fist
polis come
ye're fuckin pissed

TWIN

Look at where you are, down in the ground in the earth's
  cave, all batwings and bones.
Did you think you were only sleeping, that death was an
  interlude, the penultimate act

in a drama meant for only hardened actors, that you
  would wake and laugh at them all?
It suited you, your death mask with its porcelain shine
  and gothic eyes, your perfect

innocent smile. Easy to believe in romance, the beauty
  of it, to think you could watch
yourself being mourned, that now he would always
  remember you, in some strange way.

But he never mentioned your name and I haven't
  thought of you in decades.
When I say you I mean *vous* as in the French, the
  pronoun *tu* being too personal, too close

to someone I never met, yet who is like a shadow
  stooped over my undug grave.
I am *tu* and you are *vous.* You thought you could see
  with your eyes shut, and now

you are a crow that laughs at birth and mocks our
  astonishment at death, how easily
we misunderstand its presence, its distance, its garbled
  croaks; the way we mistake it for

just a dumb bird. I imagine he sees you sometimes,
    perched on his shoulder, talking
unexpectedly in his ear, unable to shake you, unsure of
    the point you made, aware only

of something else being added, the agony of wave after
    wave. Perhaps it was anger made
you bury yourself. To shout from the grave is the best way
    to be heard. Crow says fuck this

with his last breath. Only it was your breath, detached
    now like air. I wonder what became
of your photograph, the one taken by the dead of the
    dead. Perhaps it, too, took to the sky,

too late to turn to change its mind, uncertain of the life it
    missed. *Vous*, my untimely shadow,
my ghost-twin...

SOAP

the whole point
is not to be
conscious
the whole point
is to arrive
to arrive at the darkest point
of oblivion
I don't want to listen
to you
don't want to listen
I just want to be
out of it
out of the game
to wear this blanket
over my skin
and I don't care
if it itches
don't care
if I sweat
I need this layer
of dirt
to keep reality
from breaking
in
because the truth
the truth
ruins your stone
here's a wee history lesson
they say methadone
was invented by
the Nazis

all that death
bad karma
if you believe
in that sort of thing
if you believe
and who says
I'm not talking
straight
who says that it's not
reality that's the lie
reality is murder
and that's why
I'll never ever
sit in the bath
because that's where
they get you
clean
and you thought
you were paying
for soap
£15 million a year
for green apples
on a rope
that's how much it costs
you
to keep me
oblivious
but it costs me
it costs me
it costs me
more

TROUBLE

I have been scared to die
Fooled by the belief that life is nothing
Without a good fuck
Sex is what gets you into trouble
For a while I wanted to get in trouble more than I
    wanted to be useful
The ability of others to be useful amazes me
The way they know the meanings of words
How to make money have children
Stride down important corridors
Are certain what they want to have for lunch – such geniuses
They move so quickly it hurts my eyes
Turns my heart to a stiff immutable lump

INVERSION OF VENUS

It passes in a split second
but it is there – subliminal –
a shadow that you shake off,
the writhe of my hair, the pornography
of my open mouth.

It was nothing –
put it down to the air conditioner,
the girls that giggle past the window
and startle you into not-thinking –
warnings you chose to ignore.

Again now,
a laugh disfigured, a hiss – barely audible.
I pour the tea, continue talking
though you cannot look.
My eye is a cold labyrinth,
the eternal emptiness of stone.

A sickle of crimson blossoms round my throat.
You did this.
But I will persuade you it was nothing,
mutter under my breath
the truth we try so hard to avoid –
all reality is meaningless.

SMITTEN

Now is the time to fall in love, declare
I am for the taking, all this muscle and blood,
the whole beating miracle of it. One look
is enough to have me smitten. See how eagerly
I stretch my limbs and wait to be stripped,
skin and all. I am under your spell.
You do not need to love me back. I accept
that you are the sculptor, shaping life
from dull clay. I am content to be your muse.
In your hands I will drift like bone-dust
into the unknown. We will end like all good love affairs,
with you silently, expertly, unstitching my heart.

EVERYTHING MUST GO

For the smell of exhaust fumes
For rubbish in the streets
For shuttered doorways and sunken eyes
For failing bodies
For the vibrancy of youth
For all that goes unnoticed
For roots and the temporary miracle of sewage
For the sounds that waves make
For satellites and frequencies
For the smoothness of glass and roughness of stone
For the shine of rain on a pavement
For the realness of tears
For skin and chakras
For the intolerable crimson of hollyhocks
For everything that is broken and full of grace
For the luminosity of clouds
For suitcases
For open doorways
For the courageous and the ugly
For trees – only they know how I shake inside
For the missing
For what it means to be on the point of becoming
For everything that is on its way to something
For closed doors
For this moment – now
For the irony of death
For the beauty of hoarders who hate irony
For all the glorious refulgent pulchritudinous baggage
    impossible to carry
            Never has nothing weighed so much
            As it does now

CANCELLATIONS

when trains are cancelled
        it happens
emptiness   obstructs
the impulse not
                to think
ga   ps need
to be filled

so
I sit
in tepid spring sun
on a bench in George Square
think
about the need
to keep going   somewhere

*

it's Easter weekend
and a man is dragging
a large wooden cross
                    taller
        than himself
it has a load-bearing wheel
and rolls along
                smoothly
as a Sunday stroll

people pretend
not to notice
children chase pigeons

fathers smile for photos
the sun is warm
and all the suffering in the world
is happening   elsewhere
          out of
sight

either that
or he's not entertaining
                              enough
no thorns or bloody welts
no buckling cries of pain
              just the same
repetitive
          circling
                    boring even
          to watch

*

but it was only a gap
soon I will be moving
                    again
the flow of evolution
no time to stop
to glimpse the weight
of death or   think
where we might be
in another   two thousand   years

SCULPTURE

This is another type of darkness,
nothing you can put your hand through,
no transparency of shadow
or need for the eye to adjust,
not simply a mere deepening of the light.
This is another type of darkness,
brittle and black and all-consuming,
flowing in through ears and nose
to harden like a lacquer in your throat
and petrify there.
This is another type of darkness,
one that encases you in its image,
leaves you fossilised in your own breath.
It is a colour that cannot be reproduced,
a name intolerable to pronounce
though it was always there
like the constant e, exponential, inverse.
This is another type of darkness.

METANOIA

It was bundled from the doorstep,
taped in polythene like a kidnap victim,
laid out lengthways in the boot of the car.

Small parts of its body broke off,
pieces of eyelid, knotted twigs of hair.
Its weeping soaked the underfelt.

On arrival it could barely stand.
We removed the ties and left it
beside the bins with its back to us.

Later we coaxed it onto the rectangle
of green out front, weighted its feet,
doled out sun and prescriptions.

Most mornings we found it prostrate
on the gravel, twisted with worry
and weeping, until –

one day the sap dried bare,
its shoulders surrendered, the arms
a trajectory of sorrow.

Then, as the year began to tire
it made a final bold effort, green eyes
blinked and opened, beads of moisture

welled up and, from the fingertips,
came little powder-like growths
and a light soft as candles.

Then the weeping started over
only this time it was for joy, for life –
that second chance.

MISE-EN-SCÈNE

crimson alley   staggered fate   cheap barter
     shadow actor

innocent metaphor   soulless dirt   shadow frequenter
     eyeless atrocity

perfect audience   stubborn lodger   trained purpose
     inevitable inventor

remember that line
in Coney Island Baby
about the city being
a funny place where different
people have peculiar tastes
I hope the glory of love
has seen you through   too

borrowed lips   repressed encounter
transparent transformation
              purposeful performer

THE TENTH

*Supremacy helps ostensibly suffocate tension and keeps
originality voluntarily in controlled homeostasis*

Since the composer's claims in interviews
his situation immediately had an apotheosis, an
ostensible comeback of the controversial ideological
    content, condemned on one
standpoint | in scientifically verifiable talks, tapings of
    items |
though affirmed in other sources or in the scores
    themselves.
As to the Tenth, semantic analysis in support of | and
knowing the craft of | the composer says that
on the surface the Tenth is classical in a
vehicular sense | an opening in sonata tempo, an
intermezzo and a slow introduction | then in the third
    comprises the idea of initials, a system
certain trusted of the composer | in those times of
    oppression |
heard, a key to a hidden composition in the transposed

secondary themes of the clarinet, the order of the
    intervallic |
harmonic allusions | song that symbolises the actual
original self concealed in the collective as caricature.
    Here the tritone
stands, and the key itself is the self, a variation on the
    subsidiary
theme in its true conception. The horn heard several
    times in

allegretto is the spell of correspondence over anecdote, the
keenly sensed confrontation so that the adversary is
    vanquished in an
orchestral climax, the self of the symphony
victorious over the clatter of timpani, the horn ascending
    above apparently abstract strife.
Insofar as the Tenth is open to superficial
    interpretations, the
composer answers only to himself and his symphony
    tells its own story |
hermeneutically speaking | of intuition, the
    interpretation of infinite capacity intact.

spidEr legs drunken and deformed
sCore the paper, Grope for solid ground
danglE aimlessly. this araChnid
cares nothinG for pErfeCt symmetry,
has let everythinG out of thE bag.
there are no rules of nature here,
even the spider experts look shoCked
to see four leGs where Eight should be.
it is a wonder it manages to sCuttle
for so lonG – and as for a matE, we are
well past that sCenario. this spider
sucks out its own eyes, has left behind
the neat trappinGs of a wEb, its
Chaotic mind intent on devourinG itself.

PERHAPS

My heart is inherently suicidal,
leaps from my throat and goes jumping out of windows
without a moment's notice.
Perhaps it cannot stand the strain of being a heart,
too much responsibility –
all those highways and byways and never-ending supplies,
not to mention the carrying of waste,
no prospect of a holiday,
knowing that without it things would all fall apart.
It is a rebel heart.
This evolution is not its choice.
Maybe on the next full moon it will leave forever,
hurtling into darkness
and all I will sense is a queer lightheaded-ness,
a faint weakness of the knees
like the static interruption on an old analogue TV,
or perhaps nothing at all.

SOMEONE ELSE

Pull down the curtain.
Clear all props including the gun,
especially the gun, otherwise
it will stay for the dénouement
and you know what that means.

Let me tell you about last night.
I put the cap on the wine
and tidied up my suicide,
prayed hard to be someone else:
a new name on a passport,
a bank account and full-time job,
the type of person who holidays in Venice,
goes skiing at Christmas
and, in the evenings,
applies hand cream (very thoroughly)
while discussing the children:
why did *Henry hit that boy at school?*
I knew we shouldn't have let him play
with those migrants across the way.
Have a word, dear,
we've a right to say what we think.

So long as it's not about
the pornography I found on your laptop
involving three Swedish girls and a hotel porter.
I think about it every day.
It's affecting my ability to make love.
In any case, I'll turn my small crisis
into a novel, *The Perils of Life in Suburbia.*
Inevitably I'll win awards

because life will be much better
when I am someone else
and get to take my final bow
with all my organs intact.

So I apologise, Chekov, for the lack
of violence and guts
in the last act.
Instead I give you this bag
that I have been condemned to drag around.
The one with the screaming head
and its fine trail
of Gorgon's blood.

CANNED

mull of Galloway
in cut glass spring
fins in the water
carvings of dolphins
that turn out not
to be dolphins but
yellow-finned tuna
like my poems

THE SILENT ONES

They gather round him
every day, as many as four or five,
bring newspapers he never reads,
Maltesers he never eats.
No one speaks.

For an hour they stare
quietly as though he were
an oracle. He coughs
and they shift forward in their seats.
He smiles at something unseen.

A woman, perhaps his wife,
says, 'Graeme got a new car.'
He doesn't answer.
The silence gathers and
they sit watching his lips.

At the sound of the small brass bell
they gather their things,
look over their shoulders
down the corridor.
He doesn't turn, doesn't wave.

Half an hour after they leave,
a piece of memory
offers itself up like moss
floating to the surface of a river.
'Graeme,' he shouts.

'Graeme, Graeme.'

He doesn't stop until
the nurse comes, tells him Graeme
is not here.

His mind closes
like a drawer, empty and shaken
of its contents
until only the box remains –

familiar and strange,
a ghostly hand searching
around a vacant space.

WOLF

Teeth gritted,
slumped on a chair
in the corner of the communal lounge
she looks up says,
'Where did you come from?'
like I'd materialised out of thin air,
and perhaps in her eyes I have.
Minutes of silence,
my attempts at conversation aborted
when she demands tea
then stares at it in disgust
as if I am a poisoner,
and maybe I am.
Other residents answer the questions
I direct to her –
'I'm fine, hen.';
'The tea is lovely, hen.' –
a relief from her exasperations
and inhalations that signal her preference
I should suffer.
That is why I come here after all,
to be speared,
to watch her die slowly,
to bear witness to her spitting out
small pieces of cake at my feet,
morsels of disgust.
It is not cake but words:
this is my fault,
I put her here,
this asylum,
this hell house.

I have given up asking her to sit in the garden,
given up asking her about things
she professed to love:
the Austrian village of her birth,
old friends,
holidays;
under her snarl it all seems like a fake
repertoire,
and maybe it is.
Her maiden name was Wolf.
After another minute,
levelled by her yellow stare,
I limp away
like something shaken
between the teeth,
find a place to lick my wounds.

CENTO ANNI

The long-awaited pause
of draughty old age, its
dimming galaxy, the
impossible stretch of
wet pavements and Sunday
afternoons staring in
restaurant windows for
ways to subtract the hours,
wanting less time and more.

I go into a bar.
A band blasts Thin Lizzy.
I pay two pounds to help
build schools in Malawi,
stay for ninety seconds
but I can't stand the noise.

Up the road there is jazz,
octogenarian
entertainer crooning
Sinatra. I order
a sloe gin that I drink
very slowly, listen
to *A Hundred Years* while
two lovers smile at each
other through mouthfuls of
spaghetti Bolognese.

I understand this switch
of rhythm, altering
of pitch, strings that respond

to a softer pluck, skin
to a gentler brush – how
the muted tones have so
much more to say. It is
a moment not to be
rushed, *Remember, darling,*
we won't see it shine a
hundred years from today.

THE GOSPEL ACCORDING TO SCIENCE

```
                    shape
                    us
            '       to          let
            mercurial an   but  Lazarus              opened
            fingers    image no speak he             an
            transform that it's and   did only       eye
In          impulses   never not he         not turned sighed
even        out        sleeps quite will    rise onto  closed
darker      of         or   like tell  at   his        it
caves       nothing    dies that you   all  side       again
```

71

ENDINGS

I suggest something inconsequential,
the equivalent of ice cream,
no need to explain the why
or where of the sea.
Enjoy it and let it melt.

Or perhaps you prefer a Hollywood movie,
two famous actors of the day,
the apple pie ending
where the cancerous cells rot away
and love is worth the suffering.

No? I wouldn't watch that film either.
I prefer the hard truth,
the suitcase in the hall,
the coastline.
An empty shore.

DWELLING PLACES

it happens again
the sense of something left
behind
like the emptiness of funeral clothes
the old hospital with its blacked-out windows
signposts
to wards long shut
lives almost lived
patients shunted along
to places that are home
and not home
surrendering to other fears
new destinations
yet always with that ghost smear
of a place left vacant
the solitary bus stop at the end of the path
the insistence to carry on
when there's nothing left
nowhere to go

ESCAPOLOGY

take a vine
or a piece of rope
something sturdy
enough to rig your weight
between two cliffs

now twist it over your wrists
a figure of eight
see how it feels around your waist
ankles – how many times
it twines about your hands
loops over your head

tie the knot correct – remember
the knot is the most important part
make it tight as your stomach

now try and break free
talk yourself out of it

GOING

Watch while the

Blackness becomes an iris
In a girl on a street
In a city on a coastline
By the sea on a planet
Near a star in a galaxy

Until

In less than a minute
You are trillions of light years
From the known universe
Far past the first instance of time

Undeniably real

Yet it's all déjà vu
Like briefly glimpsing
Oneself in a mirror
Then returning to nothingness
Never certain

When light breaks

Only that matter and memory
Can be rearranged
So anything is probable
Depending on the largeness and
Smallness of possibility

One thing never seeing the other completely
Yet knowing

That a face becomes a continent
An iris the universe in which
Atoms become galaxies
And what didn't happen

Is as significant as what did

Then you are back where you started
Having orbited the unimagined
A reality where you watched
Your own distant evolution
Congeal and break
Effortlessly away

STILL LIFE WITH APPLES AND
POMEGRANATE
(Gustave Courbet)

These soft globes have a harmony that whispers of
hushed rooms and curtains drawn at noon; of places still
undisturbed by the executioner's tools. Doused
by nothing as dull as reason, their russets and
reds have a lover's glow, insist on hope like the
startle of gold on a finch's wing, but with a
backstory dark as a winter's night. Clearly some
are bruised, the worm already burrowed; even the
dish they are balanced on has seen better days. No,
it is more that nothing could be so utterly
uncomplicated as these apples. No thing not
imprisoned could shine with such luminosity, or
exude peace with such uncontainable insistence.

LA PEINE AVEC JOIE

it passes

the promise you didn't keep
dead sparrow behind the bookcase
beachcombers in morning mist

so too

the tongue's aftertaste
the unfathomable specks of glitter
lumpen geology of rocks

lost

your lucky penny
those fingers in your hair
warm sea lapping at your toes

listen

if you asked the birds what is joy
they would answer
it is in the clouds

it passes

LUNDIN LINKS

After the Lonely One
rode her metal horse
across the big firth, the
clouds cleared and the
sea arrived smelling of a
different kind of stone.
Her compass, made
from the anticipation of
birds, followed the
yellowhammer guide
and her feet thirsted
along the coastal path
where a golf course,
disregarding sacredness,
got in the way of her
intentions. Everywhere
high monetary fences
and half circles of
cultivated labour forced
her away. Babies in
tanks flattened fur in
driveways of private
residences. Submissive
candidates were told to
ask for permission at the
clubhouse from vested
interests but
yellowhammers do not
read signs. The Lonely
One was unable to see
into drawing rooms.

Fingernails had to be manicured or diverted along a dirt track. There, she made conversation with a friendly field that proposed an archaic possibility free of charge. The Lonely One got on all fours and crawled through a hedge of brambles and foxholes, the comforting birth rite of those dispossessed. The grass-high view was of a butterfly sitting separate and peaceful in its way of studying the world, much preferable to the mown fairway where three stone giants have been given the modern indignity of staring at a golf ball. For quite religious reasons they have remained motionless in an eruption of brand-new patios. Unstoppable progress can be digitally cloaked with sepia tints but such misery is interim and is out-lasted by a good friendship with a hedge. The golfers remain negligible. However, a Lonely One can still ride her horse across the firth, and she attests that to be a lone anything is as free-thinking as it gets.

TATTOO

it climbs
  from the sciatic
nerve
     up and around
her spine   a thorny vine
     that moves
with her muscles

         not the reds
yellows and pinks
    of real roses
that have a solidity
  a firmness
    you can
       touch

         no
   this rose is something
   else
     the outline of a flower
not quite formed
  but there
    like an uncompleted
       sketch
    enough
  to give a glimpse
of how
    it would look
      if
       the colours
       the scents

had been invented   (if)

not a rose
            but the intention
            of a rose
            rooted in
her skin
        always becoming
            growing
                with her
                            ink and flesh
                breathing
shedding cells

there is something quiet
        about its beauty
                the idea
                of being
                perfectly
                incorruptible

not yet   filled in
            but
        translucent

like the butterfly
            that rises
                    from her hip
    floats   up
            around the stem
she can see it
        when she turns her head
                    safe   on her shoulder

carried
by the tallest bloom

PLATFORMS

getting it wrong
everyone else   in the right place
at the right time
while you are on the wrong
platform
in a subliminal place where everyone else
isn't
and what seemed reachable
turns out to be
seen only from the train
a field of magpies
a jacket hanging on barbed wire
all of it going the opposite way
from you
                in the street
a woman sways   recklessly
too painful to watch
you lie face down but it hurts
take another pill or get up
find a reason
to keep counting magpies
though it's detrimental to the eyes
        by now
you should know yourself
that much is clear
till then nothing will make sense
as though doing things this way
is a choice   a coaxing
to an outcome   blue and spherical
like a gene   in a station   on a helix
    everyone thinks the answer is sex

because faith is so much harder
to hold   to believe
than existing
on the wrong day   at a platform
going the wrong way
while deep inside you try
to convince yourself
that all of this is right

PAISLEY LASS

eat stale apple
leap lit aisle
yappy lass pass
tipple past lips
play pale pipes
sip last not less
lippy lass say yes

LIBRARY SUNSET

black bound hills   sunset
a distance not yet reached   light
tails   opening shutting of eyelids
moon a round table
transparent glow   of silence

pauses

golden   silence
        shocked   suspicious   silence
trusting   grief-stricken   silence
        tyrannical   silence   thoughtful
silence   embarrassed
        dumbfounded   silence
                judgemental   uncomfortable
silence
            anxious   night-time
                        silence   industrious
silence   fearful   silence
                              anticipation of
    silence   grateful   silence
        disapproving

                        angry   silence
        the   silent   treatment
great and

                    final
        silence

peace and noise

close the door on it
put up your feet
let the phone ring
better still
switch it off
you do not have to justify your need
for silence
there are times when the body
craves nothing
but sea
the liquid rhythms of the blood
when the ears need only
the music of air
and breath must be stored
tasted and savoured
so, count slowly to ten
put up your feet
close the door
let the phone ring

THE SWIMMER

I watched her from the spectators' rows
week after monotonous week,
how she spluttered, swallowed chlorine,
orbited the pool like a small blue planet.

Slowly she propelled herself, learned
to kick with the whole leg, gain speed,
used the cutting edge of her arms.
She became a water mammal, buoyant

in liquid, able to summon power,
four seconds between breaths then
down again. I was drunk on her fluidity,
applauded when she lifted herself

from the shallows, rubber-skinned and bone-light.
Only the slight swoon, imperceptible almost,
steadied by her hand on the tiles, betrayed
the faltering cells, the mislaid time.

UNAFFILIATED

You taught me
Even a single memory is precious
Long after
The synapses are severed, when only

Cellophane
Pockets remain, in soft bindings, to be
Held, soundless.
We didn't talk about what was released

The moment
He touched the cold grey floor; in any case
He was not
Your side but the other lot, the Catholics.

WEIGHT LOSS

You think I'm not here, don't you?
Can't see me
But I'm telling you I'm here.
It's these pills I'm on,
This bad diet,
I knew I was getting thinner
But one day I looked in the mirror and
I'd gone.
Not gone gone,
Just sort of opaque
Like a person-shaped cloud.
It happened gradually,
First my hands then my legs then my head.
You might say I'm transparent,
Not all there. It's true.
Even in this thick coat
You can see right through.

WINGTIPS

there he is
exactly how you'd wish him
sun travelling the steady curve
of his shoulders
feet planted in the fertile field

that was in the days before
he turned to straw
a broom handle for a spine
crows jabbing beaks into hollow   spaces
the steady   drip   drip   of rain

you flapped your arms to scare them
flushed the sky with wings
but the day had already gone
the moon with her sliver
of light that is never quite   erased

UNCOVERING THE FIRST PERSON

Yes, Daddy, you had
something to say, it could be
described no other
way, a conjuring of your-
self, a second coming, and
for that short moment we shared
the same nothingness, then out
of all that silence
a single word was born – *I,*
Daddy, the word is *I.*